The New Novello Choral Edition

LUDWIG VAN BEETHOVEN

Mass in C

for SATB soli, choir and orchestra

Vocal score

Revised by Michael Pilkington

Order No: NOV 078562

NOVELLO PUBLISHING LIMITED

It is requested that on all concert notices and programmes acknowledgement is made to 'The New Novello Choral Edition'.

Es wird gebeten, auf sämtlichen Konzertankündigungen und Programmen 'The New Novello Choral Edition' als Quelle zu erwähnen.

Il est exigé que toutes notices et programmes de concerts, comportent des remerciements à 'The New Novello Choral Edition'.

Orchestral material is available on hire from the Publisher.

Orchestermaterial ist beim Verlag erhältlich.

Les partitions d'orchestre sont en location disponibles chez l'editeur.

Permission to reproduce the Preface of this Edition must be obtained from the Publisher.

Die Erlaubnis, das Vorwort dieser Ausgabe oder Teile desselben zu reproduzieren, muß beim Verlag eingeholt werden.

Le droit de reproduction de ce document à partir de la préface doit être obtenu de l'éditeur.

© 2002 Novello & Company Limited

Exclusive distributors:

Hal Leonard
7777 West Bluemound Road, Milwaukee, WI 53213
Email: info@halleonard.com

Hal Leonard Europe Limited
42 Wigmore Street Maryleborne, London, WIU 2 RY
Email: info@halleonardeurope.com

Hal Leonard Australia Pty. Ltd.
4 Lentara Court Cheltenham, Victoria, 9132 Australia
Email: info@halleonard.com.au

Music setting by Engima Music Production Services

PREFACE

Beethoven's Mass in C was commissioned by Prince Nikolaus Esterházy for the name-day of his wife, Princess Maria, and was first performed on 13 September 1807. Beethoven's setting continues the series of six great Masses composed by Haydn in previous years for the same occasion. Most of the autograph score is missing and the first edition was published by Breitkopf & Härtel in 1812.

The edition of this work found in the Complete Works Series 19 (published by Breitkopf & Härtel between 1862 and 1865) contains a large number of editorial additions in the way of slurs and dynamics when compared with the first edition, though none of these additions has been marked as such.

The present edition is based on the first edition, with all editorial emendations from the Complete Works marked with square brackets and strokes through slurs and hairpins. The occasional use of round brackets shows dynamics added by the editor. These markings have all been added to the full score.

Sources:
A   First edition, Breitkopf & Härtel, 1812.
B   Complete Works Series 19, Breitkopf & Härtel, c. 1864.

NOTES
Kyrie
Bar 44
The chorus altos have only a quaver in **A**, perhaps to give the alto soloist, who would have been a member of the chorus, more time for a breath before her entry at the end of the bar.

Gloria
Bar 136-7
It appears that in manuscript sources the second violins continued in octaves with the first violins to the end of bar 137, which was clearly an error. **A** has the second violins in unison with the firsts for notes 2-4 of bar 136, and nothing in bar 137. The solution given here and in **B** seems the simplest.

Credo
Bars 323, 324
The first note for bassoons and violas in bar 323 is c′ in **B**, but the b♭ of **A** is clearly correct; on the other hand **B**'s correction of **A**'s f″ for the fourth note of the second violins is certainly right.
Bars 334-5
For some reason these two bars are blank for the basses in **B**, but this Amen is given in **A**.
Bar 337
A gives the first note for the second violins as c″, and for violas e′. However, the version in **B** seems reasonable, and is retained here.
Bar 339
Soprano note 3 is given as c″ in both **A** and **B**, but see oboe 1.

Sanctus.
Bar 6 beat 3 - bar 9; written in sharps in **A**, the enharmonic change to flats in **B** is easier to read, and is retained.

Benedictus.
Bar 3. The cello part is marked 'Solo' in **A**, though not in **B**. Strangely, Willy Hess in his Eulenberg edition of 1964 does not give 'solo', but throughout his critical notes to this passage he refers to 'Solo cello'.
Bar 34, alto, 35, tenor: **B** has moved '- mi -' from note 5, as given in **A**, to note 7 in both cases.

Agnus Dei
Bars 17-18
The wind parts are confused in **A**, the solution in **B** is followed here.

Michael Pilkington
Old Coulsdon 2002

MASS IN C

KYRIE

*Alto: see Preface

4

GLORIA

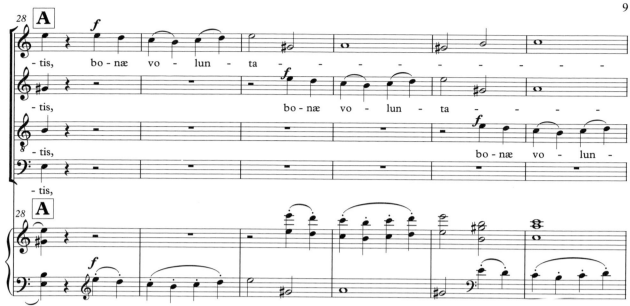

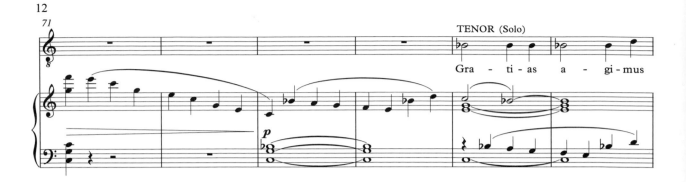

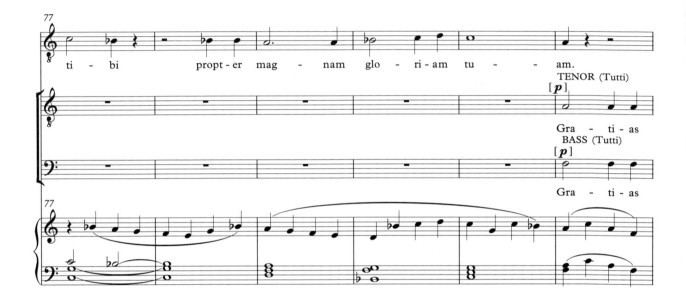

*Bar 87, beat 1: f in **A**

89

Do- - - - mi - ne De - us, Rex cœ - les - tis, De - us

tu - am.

tu - am.

tu - am.

tu - am.

95

Pa - ter om - ni - po - tens. Do - - mi - ne

Tutti *f*
De - us om - ni - po - tens.

Tutti *f*
De - us om - ni - po - tens.

Tutti *f*
De - us om - ni - po - tens.

Tutti *f*
De - us om - ni - po - tens.

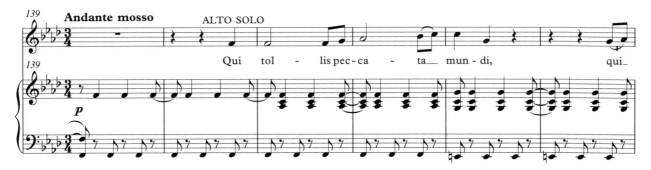

18

*Beat 3: upper three notes missing in **A**

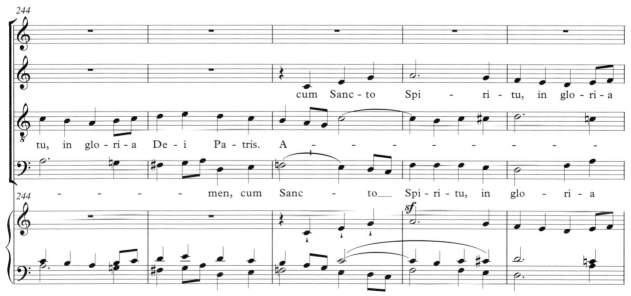

24

*Bar 295, Tenor note 1: octave lower in **A**

Spi - ri - tu, in glo - ri - a De - i Pa - tris. A -
Spi - ri - tu, in glo - ri - a De - i Pa - tris. A -
cum Sanc - to Spi - ri - tu, in glo - ri - a De - i Pa - tris.
cum Sanc - to Spi - ri - tu, in glo - ri - a De - i Pa - tris.

- men. A -
- men.
A - men.
A - men.

- men, a -

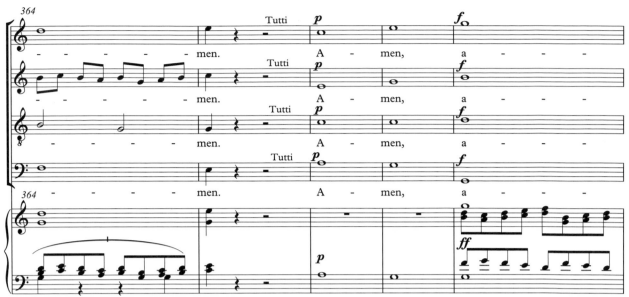

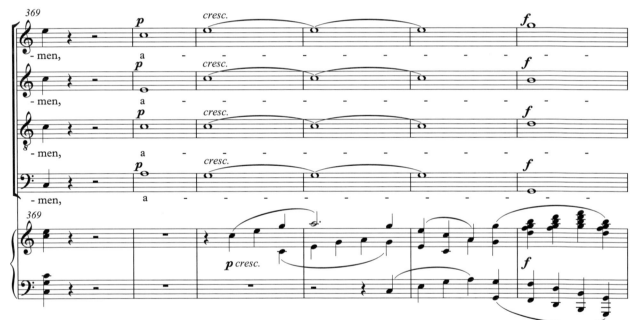

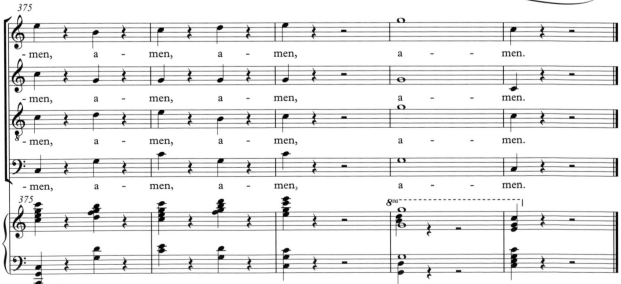

CREDO

35

36

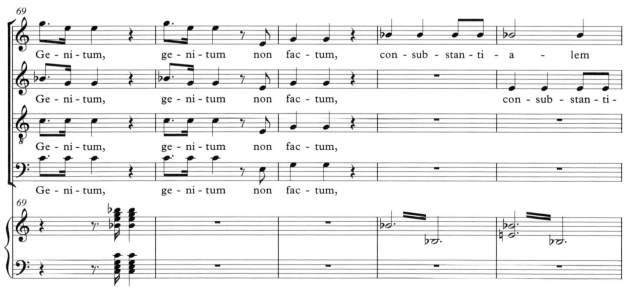

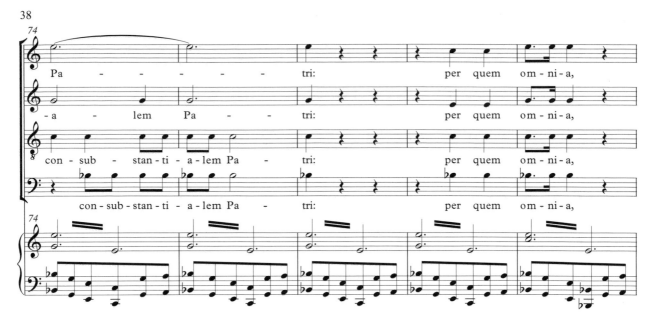

*Beat 1, RH rhythm: ♪ ♪ in **A**

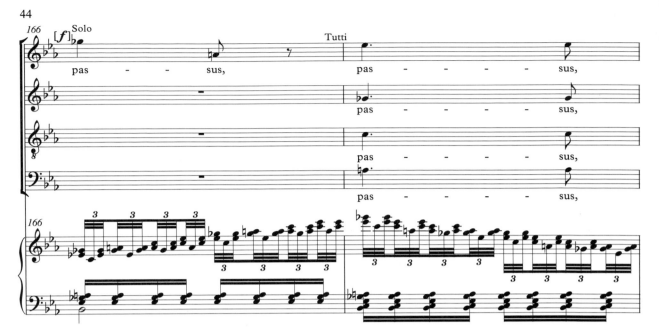

*Bass solo: ♯ to 2nd C in **A**

47

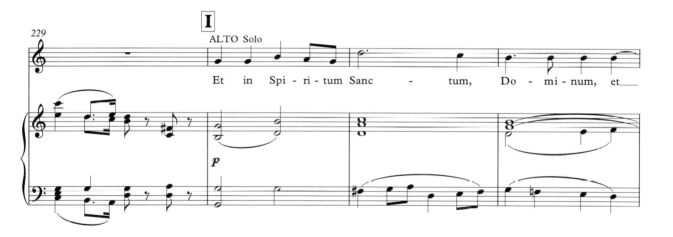

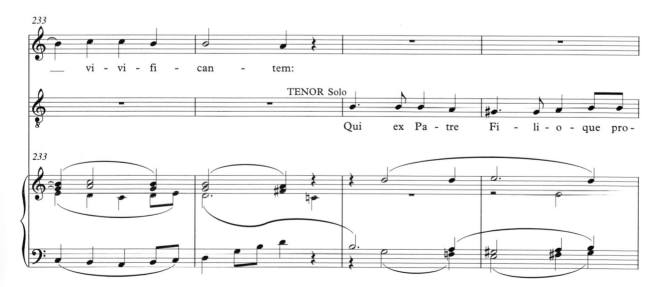

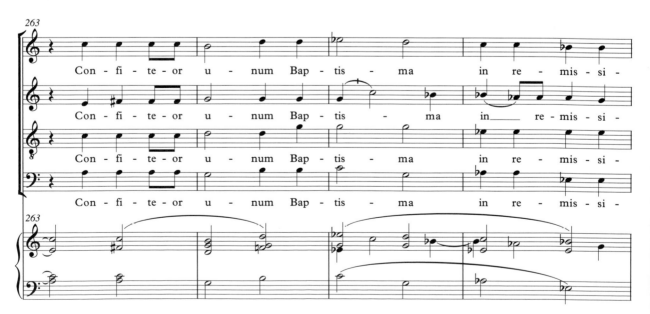

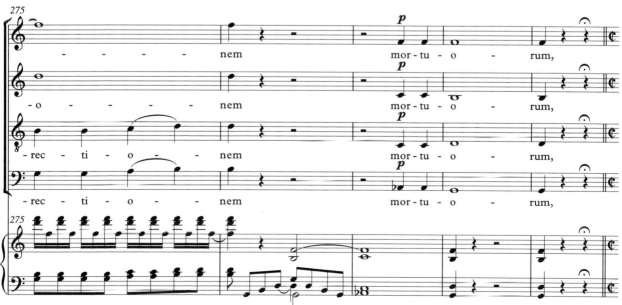

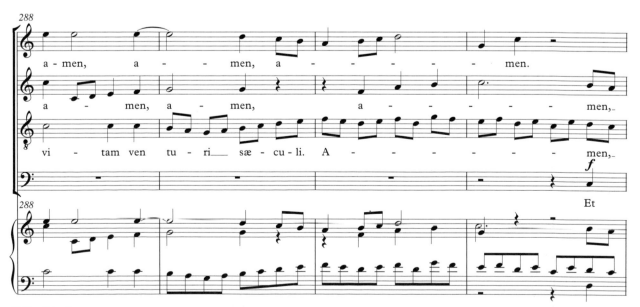

*¢ for ¢ in A

58

* see Preface
†solo note 3: c" in **A**, **B**

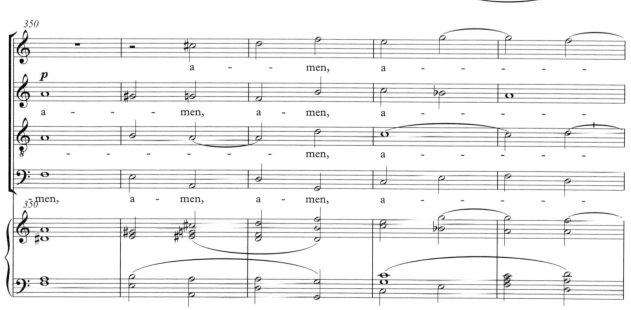

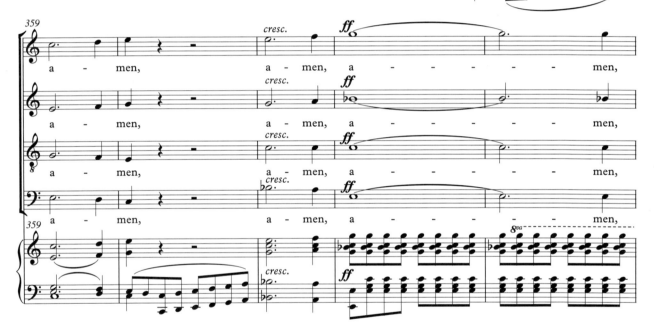

SANCTUS

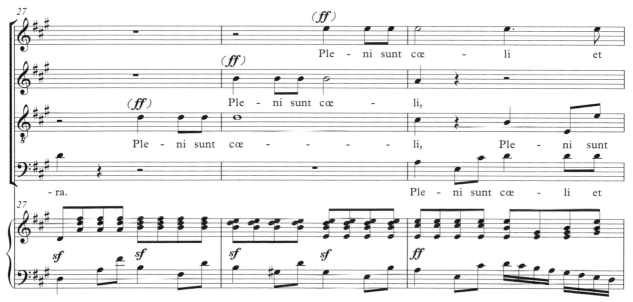

*Tenor note 2: g for f in **A**

64

BENEDICTUS

* see Preface

*Alternatives given by the composer.

*Alternatives given by the composer.

AGNUS DEI

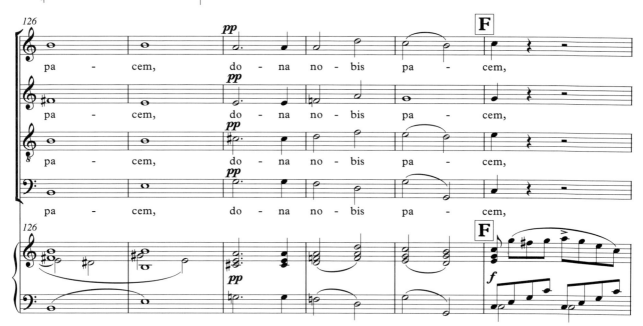

NOVELLO REVISED STANDARD CHORAL EDITION

Fully revised and edited performing versions of many of the major works in the large-scale choral concert repertoire, replacing the standard Novello editions, often putting back the composers' intentions, restoring the original text, modernised accompaniments and providing new English translations.

Orchestral material, where necessary, is available on hire.

J.S. BACH
(ed. Neil Jenkins)

Ascension Oratorio
NOV090860
German and English text

Christmas Oratorio
NOV072500
German and English text

Easter Oratorio
NOV090849
German and English text

Magnificat in D and E♭
NOV072529
German and English text in the four
Lauds in the E♭ version

Mass in B minor
NOV078430

St. John Passion
NOV072489
German and English text

St. Matthew Passion
NOV072478
German and English text

BEETHOVEN
(ed. Michael Pilkington)

Choral Finale to the Ninth Symphony
NOV072490
German and English text

Mass in C
NOV078562

Missa Solemnis (Mass in D)
NOV072497

BRAHMS
(ed. Pilkington)

A German Requiem
NOV072492
German and English text

DVOŘÁK
(ed. Pilkington)

Mass in D NOV072491
Requiem NOV072516
Stabat Mater NOV072503
Te Deum NOV078573

ELGAR
(ed. Bruce Wood)

The Dream of Gerontius
NOV072530

Great Is the Lord
NOV078595

GOUNOD
(ed. Pilkington)

Messe solennelle de Sainte Cécile
NOV072495

HANDEL

Belshazzar
(ed. Donald Burrows) NOV070530

Four Coronation Anthems
NOV072507
 The King Shall Rejoice
 (ed. Damian Cranmer)
 Let Thy Hand be Strengthened
 (ed. Burrows)
 My Heart is Inditing *(ed. Burrows)*
 Zadok the Priest *(ed. Burrows)*

Judas Maccabaeus
(ed. Merlin Channon)
NOV072486

The King Shall Rejoice
(ed. Cranmer) NOV072496

Let Thy Hand be Strengthened
(ed. Burrows) NOV072509

Messiah
(ed. Watkins Shaw) NOV070137
 Study Score NOV890031

My Heart is Inditing
(ed. Burrows) NOV072508

O Praise the Lord
(from Chandos Anthem No. 9)
(ed. Graydon Beeks) NOV072511

This Is the Day
(ed. Hurley) NOV072510

Zadok the Priest
(ed. Burrows) NOV290704

HAYDN
(ed. Pilkington)

The Creation
NOV072485
German and English text

The Seasons
NOV072493
German and English text

Te Deum Laudamus
NOV078463

"Maria Theresa" Mass
NOV078474

Mass "In Time of War"
NOV072514

"Nelson" Mass
NOV072513

"Wind Band" Mass
(Harmoniemesse)
NOV078507

MAUNDER

Olivet to Calvary
NOV072487

MENDELSSOHN
(ed. Pilkington)

Elijah
NOV070201
German and English text

Hymn of Praise
NOV072506

MONTEVERDI
(ed. Denis Stevens)

Gloria in excelsis
NOV078551

MOZART

Requiem
(ed. Duncan Druce) NOV070529

Coronation Mass
(Mass in C K.317)
(ed. Pilkington) NOV072505

Mass in C minor
(reconstr. Philip Wilby) NOV078452

PURCELL

Come, Ye Sons of Art, Away
(ed. Wood) NOV072467

Welcome to All the Pleasures
(ed. Wood) NOV290674

Ed. Vol. 15 Royal Welcome Songs 1
(ed. Wood) NOV151118

Ed. Vol. 22A Catches
(ed. Ian Spink) NOV151103

ROSSINI

Petite messe solennelle
NOV072436

SCHUBERT

Mass in G, D.167 (SSA version)
NOV070258

SCHÜTZ
(ed. Jenkins)

Christmas Story
NOV072525
German and English text

STAINER
(ed. Pilkington)

The Crucifixion
NOV072488

VERDI
(ed. Pilkington)

Requiem
NOV072403

VIVALDI
(ed. Jasmin Cameron)

Gloria
NOV078441